ODEON

PRAGA CAPUT REGNI

THE SIGHTS OF PRAGUE AND ITS NEIGHBORHOOD

KAREL NEUBERT

JAN ROYT

ODEON

Karel Neubert
Jan Royt
The Sights of Prague and Its Neighborhood

Artists and visitors alike claim Prague as one of the most beautiful cities in the world. Prague's position in the heart of Bohemia and thousand--year-long history make it the natural capital of the Czech and Slovak Federative Republic.

The central artery of the territory on which the city lies is the Vltava river, into which smaller rivers and streams flow from the surrounding hills and valleys. The massive formation of the Maiden's Castles and Barrandov Rock form the gateway to the city on the Vltava's left bank. The rock is named after French palaeontologist Joachim Barrande, who discovered imprints and fossils of long extinct organisms in the primary slate rocks here. Smíchov, an industrial area of Prague, rises above Újezd to the steep Petřín hill, bordered by the fortifications, known, since the time of the Emperor Charles, as the Hunger Wall. From here Malá Strana (Little Quarter), Hradčany and the ramparts of Letná ascend, further on giving way to the industrial area of Holešovice and then Vysočany.

On the right bank, opposite Barrandov, the mighty cliff of Vyšehrad towers over the river, centuries after its ancient castle was demolished. Between the cliff and Vítkov sits the historic core of Prague, Staré Město (the Old Town) and Nové Město (the New Town). Rising above them are two districts built in the 19th century, Vinohrady and Žižkov. Below Vítkov lies Karlín, also originating in the 19th century.

The urban agglomeration of Prague also includes residential areas like Hanspaulka and Baba, and extensive suburban housing developments such as the Southern and Northern Towns. Over two hundred adjoining districts and hamlets have become part of Greater Prague, which now covers an area of more than 500 km^2 populated by some 1,300,000 inhabitants.

Archeologists have traced the settlement of Prague back to neolithic times. As early as the 9th century, following a brief period when the House of Přemyslides in Levý Hradec served as the administrative and ecclesiastical centre for the Czech tribe, Prague became the centre of the emerging state of Bohemia. According to legend, the first mythical princes and later kings of the House of Přemyslides resided at Vyšehrad. But the seat of the Přemyslides later crossed the river to the site where the Prague Castle stands today. Here the first secular and sacred buildings were erected: the little church of Our Lady, the rotunda tetraconch of St. Vitus and the Prince's Palace. The basilica of St. George and the first convent of Benedictine nuns in Bohemia were built between the 9th and 12th centuries in Romanesque style. During the reign of Prince Soběslav the whole castle was surrounded by stone fortifications. There also stood within these walls the seat of the Prague bishop, named metropolitain of the country in 973.

After the death of the last Přemyslide king, Wenceslas III (1306), the House of Luxemburg ascended to the Bohemian throne (1310—1436). Under John of Luxemburg Prague's glory faded, the castle becoming a ruin. The time of greatest prosperity for both the castle and the city came under the reign of the Emperor Charles IV (1346—1378), who made Prague castle the seat of the whole empire and promoted Prague's bishopric to an archbishopric in 1344. Charles had a whole compound of palaces built within the castle walls. In 1344 he commissioned the French architect Matthias of Arras to build the new cathedral church. But Matthias died before it was completed and was replaced in 1356 by the masterly Peter Parléř (died 1399), whose company also erected the splendid palace chapel of All Saints that is reminiscent of the French Sainte-Chapelle. The beautifully decorated chapel of the greatest patron saint of the Bohemian kingdom, St. Wenceslas, became the centre of the cathedral, where the Bohemian crown jewels are kept along with many valuable relics. The cathedral also served as the burial grounds for Bohemian kings and Prague archbishops. During the Hussite wars (1415—1434) the castle was damaged and the other royal seat, Vyšehrad, completely destroyed.

The Prague Castle next flourished during the reign of the Polish House of Jagellons (1471—1526). The prevalent architectural style was the dynamic Late Gothic, which produced the monumental Vladislav Hall (1493), whose windows show hints of an emerging Renaissance style, and also the Old Diet and the royal chambers.

With the ascent of the Habsburgs, who ruled in Bohemia from 1526 until 1918, Italian Renaissance architecture found its way to Bohemia. The earliest example of this style north of the Alps is Queen Anne's summer palace, Belvedere. Another remarkable Renaissance building is the Ball Court in the Prague Castle gardens. In 1541 fire destroyed a large part of the castle.

Emperor Rudolph II (1576—1612) gathered leading European Mannerist artists, astronomers and alchemists to his court. His collections of works of art, objects of natural history and scientific instruments were famous, though the great majority of them were stolen by the Swedes at the end of the Thirty Years' War (1648). Golden Lane in the Castle, with its charming little houses for the court servants, dates from Rudolph's time. The kingdom's leading families, Rožmberks, Pernštejns and Lobkowiczes, also built palaces in the Castle grounds. Rudolph's death put an end to Prague's time as the seat of the Habsburg monarchs and the Castle lost many of its patrons. Extensive building repairs were made only under the Empress Maria Theresa at the end of the 18th century. Pacassi's late baroque renovations unified the structures of the Prague Castle that had been growing together organically over eight centuries. The Castle was then renovated in 1919 when it became the seat of the first president of free Czechoslovakia, T. G. Masaryk. The Castle buildings were adapted to the president's needs by architect Josip Plečnik. Over the past 40 years many of the buildings have been turned into exhibition halls. Czech art from the 14th to 18th centuries is exhibited in St. George's convent; the Prague Castle picture gallery has been installed in what used to be Ferdinand's and Rudolph's stables; documents from the thousand-year-long history of the nation are kept in the Lobkowicz palace.

In the Castle's immediate neighborhood lies Hradčany, a town founded at the beginning of the 14th century and once administered from Hradčany Town Hall. Nearby are the late baroque Archbishop's palace and the Šternberk palace which house the National Gallery's collection of European art. There are many architecturally valuable buildings in Hradčany Square, dominated by a Marian Column by the Czech baroque sculptor F. M. Brokof. The Renaissance Schwarzenberg palace is the site of the Military History Museum; the Martinic palace, its facade decorated with figural graffiti, serves as the office of Prague's chief architect. The little church of St. Benedict in the square holds the relics of the Beatified Electa, a Carmelite nun who came to Prague in the 17th century.

The lovely building of the Loretto with its famous chimes and church treasure, the simple structure of the Capuchin monastery, containing a unique Bethlehem crib from the 18th century, and the imposing facade of the Černín palace on Loretto Square are outstanding examples of the artistic and spiritual values of Czech baroque, a style which, together with Gothic, has given Prague its inimitable genius loci. Not far from Loretto Square, a romantic winding little street called Nový svět (the New World) breathes a nostalgic atmosphere of times gone by. Towering above Pohořelec is the immense complex of the Strahov monastery, founded in the 12th century by the Premonstratensians. The Strahov library is renowned for its halls from the late baroque period. A path leads from Strahov to Petřín hill with its Eiffel-Tower-like viewtower, built for the Jubilee World Exhibition at the end of the 19th century. Near it is a mirrored maze in the form of a medieval castle for children to play in and the pilgrimage church of St. Lawrence.

The ramp of Prague Castle affords a magnificient view of the whole city. On its slope is Malá Strana, a town founded in 1257 by King Přemysl Ottakar II. At its centre is Malá Strana Square, dominated by the church of St. Nicholas, built in high baroque style by Christopher and Kilian Ignatius Dientzenhofer for the Jesuits. The square is surrounded by Renaissance (the Šternberk palace, the Town Hall) and baroque (the Kaiserštejn) palaces. Along Neruda Street, winding down from the Castle, we find the Thun and Morzini palaces and the Theatin church, all works of the baroque architect Giovanni Santini. Parallel to it is Vlašská (Italian) Street where the Italian hospital once served the many Italian artists and craftsmen settled in Prague. Beside it are the baroque Lobkowicz and Colloredo palaces. Continuing down towards Újezd we find the Vrtba palace and its beautiful garden holding baroque statues by Matthias Bernard Braun. Further on, inside the baroque church of Our Lady Victorious, the world famous wax statue of the miraculous Prague Infant Jesus graces the side altar. The rooms of the Great Prior's palace, next door to the early Gothic church of the Johannites, house the collection of the Music Museum. Over towards Klárov are a number of precious baroque buildings and gardens, built for imperial general Albrecht of Valdštejn in the first third of the 17th century, and St. Thomas' monastery, a structure rebuilt in the baroque style by Kilian Ignatius Dientzenhofer (the picture on the high altar is a work of Peter Paul Rubens).

The medieval Karlův most (Charles Bridge) links Malá Strana and Staré Město. It was opened in 1357 to replace the ruined 12th century Romanesque Judith Bridge. The statues decorating the bridge are the works of leading Czech baroque sculptors (F. M. Brokof, M. B. Braun among others) and the subjects (patron saints of the Czech lands, saints of the orders, patrons of the university) pay tribute to their sponsors. A little cross with five stars on the balustrade of the bridge marks the place where the patron of the Czech lands, St. John of Nepomuk, was thrown into the Vltava at the end of the 14th century.

The Staré Město bridge gateway dates from the end of the 14th century. It is decorated with statues from Peter Parléř's workshop that glorify Emperor Charles IV and his son Wenceslas IV. Passing through it we enter the Square of the Knights of the Cross, one of the most delightful places in Prague. There stand the baroque church of St. Francis and the Jesuit early baroque church of St. Saviour, whose entablature is decorated with statues by Jan Jiří Bendl.

Karlova Street, along which the coronation processions of the Bohemian kings in the Middle Ages made their way from Vyšehrad to Prague Castle, crosses a cobweb of little streets where many of the houses have Romanesque foundations and leads to the centre of the Old Town: Staroměstské náměstí (Old Town Square).

Prague's Old Town, like Prague Castle and Vyšehrad, began to take shape in the 9th and 10th centuries. A report from the Jewish merchant Ibrahim Ibn Jakub from the 10th century confirms that at that time Prague's houses and churches were already built of stone. An example of such a house is the cellar (originally the ground floor) of a house on Huss Street, now the exhibition hall of the Central Bohemian Gallery. From the Old Town Hall, both the city of Prague and the Czech Lands were administered. In 1458 George of Poděbrady was elected king of Bohemia here. But the Town Hall has also witnessed many tragic events in the history of the Czech nation. In 1621 twenty-seven Czech noblemen and burghers were executed by the walls of the Town Hall for taking part in the anti-Habsburg rising that sparked off the Thirty Years' War. The building has been repaired and adapted many times since the 14th century. Its famous horloge was added in the 15th century, with figures of the apostles, the symbolic figures of the Virtues and the Vices, and a calendar panel by Josef Mánes, the best known 19th century Czech painter. An early baroque Marian Column by J. J. Bendl, built in 1650 to commemorate the end of the Thirty Years' War, once dominated the centre of the square but was destroyed in 1918. The memorial to Master John Huss, an important church reformer of the end of the 14th and beginning of the 15th centuries, still stands. His legacy is carried on by the Czechoslovak Hussite church, whose main place of worship is the baroque church of St. Nicholas in Staroměstské náměstí, built by Christopher Ignatius Dientzenhofer. The catholic church, Our Lady of Týn, was built near the oldest part of the Old Town, Ungelt or the customs house. The Parléř workshop decorated part of the church, including the magnificient northern portal. The interior holds gems of Gothic sculpture such as the Madonna of Týn and the Calvary, and baroque paintings by Karel Škréta. The Emperor Rudolph II's court astronomer, Tycho de Brahe, is buried here. In front of the church is a row of houses with medieval foundations called the Týn school. One, the House at the Sign of the Bell, was recently restored to approximate the form it had at the beginning of the 14th century. Next to it is the Kinský palace, now used for exhibitions by the National Gallery. The oldest Gothic building of the Old Town is the double monastery of the Franciscans and Poor Clares on the embankment called Na Františku, in which its foundress, St. Agnes, lived. The monastery, recently restored to house collections of 19th century Czech art, proves that the Gothic style penetrated Prague even before the middle of the 13th century. The Jewish ghetto, now known as Josefov, also dates back to medieval Prague and its famous Old-New Synagogue, one of the oldest in Europe, still stands today. The beginnings of the Jewish cemetary are also very ancient.

In the Middle Ages dozens of churches and monasteries were erected in the Old Town. In 1348 Emperor Charles IV founded Charles University not far from Staroměstské náměstí, and the famous preacher from the Bethlehem Chapel in the Old Town, Master John Huss, taught there. At the beginning of the 15th century his teachings ignited the Hussite revolution. The Prague towns, together with the south Bohemian town of Tábor, led the revolution. This marked the end of the great stage of Prague's development under Charles IV and his son Wenceslas IV, who made the city one of the biggest and most important metropolises of the world. Under the rule of the Jagellons and later the Habsburgs the prestige of the Prague towns declined and very little new building was accomplished. The Czech Utraquists, Lutherans and Calvinists, who dominated the religious life of the country in the 15th and 16th centuries, did not need new sacred buildings. The development of the Jewish town was comparatively undisturbed. New synagogues such as the Pinkas, High and Maisel synagogues, were built at the end of the 16th century. Rabbi Löw ben Bezalel Jehuda, the famous creator of Golem, lived and taught in this time and Jews from all over the world still place pebbles on his tombstone in the old cemetary today. In the 20th century most of the synagogues were converted by the State Jewish Museum to exhibit Jewish art.

Prague underwent a radical change in the 17th and 18th centuries, when many churches and houses were renovated in a baroque style. Since then the squares have been decorated with many baroque statues and fountains. The 19th century considerably changed the face of the Old Town as much of the Jewish quarter Josefov and the northern front of Staroměstské náměstí were demolished. New structures, including some important cultural buildings, were also put up at this time. By the beginning of the 19th century the stone building of the Estates Theatre, in which Mozart first conducted his opera Don Giovanni, was completed. The Rudolfinum, the Industrial Arts Museum and the High School of Industrial Arts in Palach Square were built in historic styles. From the end of the 19th to the beginning of the 20th century a number of structures, including the Municipal House, were renovated in the Art Nouveau style.

The city of Prague was greatly enlarged during the reign of Emperor Charles IV. In 1348 he founded the Nové Město (New Town) of Prague with many monasteries and squares, trying to turn Prague into "a second Rome".

Charles Square marked the centre of the New Town and in the middle of it stood the central chapel of Corpus Christi where the kingdom's most valuable relics were exhibited at church festivals. The New Town Hall in Charles Square was the administrative centre. The Jesuit College and the church of St. Ignatius were built in the 17th and 18th centuries. The house of the legendary Dr. Faust has been immortalized by German romantic writers. Charles IV founded the monastery of the Slavonic Benedictines—Emmaus—, who pursued the heritage of St. Cyril and Methodius, developed Slavonic learning, and cultivated Old Church Slavonic in the liturgy. Evidence of the cultural standards of the monastery remains in the high quality murals in the cloisters. The Rheims Gospel, on which the French kings made their coronation vows in Rheims, originated here. Close by, the church of St. John of Nepomuk on the Rock was built by Kilian Ignatius Dientzenhofer.

Leaving the square in the direction of Vyšehrad, we come to the church of the Order of Servants of the Blessed Mary, built under Charles IV and remarkable for its arched nave on a single column. Charles also commissioned the church of Our Lady and Charlemagne in Karlov, whose central polygonal nave recalls the palace chapel of Charles the Great in Aachen. In the 17th and 18th centuries this church was an important pilgrimage stop, especially for pregnant women who entreated the painting of the Virgin Mary of Karlov. The church of Our Lady of the Snows was to have been the biggest church of the town but was never completed. The church that stands today is really only the presbytery of the church building that was originally intended. Other New Town churches, such as St. Gastulus and St. Stephen, owe their medieval form to Charles IV.

After the towns of Prague were unified in 1784, the centre moved to Wenceslas Square. The building of the National Museum in 1885—1890 and the memorial to St. Wenceslas by J. V. Myslbek to replace a smaller baroque equestrian statue of the saint by Jan Jiří Bendl highlighted its new importance. In the 1870s the whole nation contributed money to build the neorenaissance National Theatre that dominates the Masaryk Embankment.

Prague's industrial activity surged in the 19th century, concentrated particularly in suburbs like Smíchov. New bridges, railway viaducts and stations were built. The new districts, built as independent towns, were later incorporated into Greater Prague.

At the beginning of the 20th century a large number of German speaking people lived in Prague, including many important writers who contributed to the city's fame. Among them was Franz Kafka, whose grave in the Jewish cemetary in Olšany is often visited.

After 1918 Czechoslovakia became a centre of European trade and culture. In the years between 1918 and 1938 Prague developed as the capital of a free, democratic state and the seat of many political, economic and cultural institutions. The Czech functional architects (Jan Kotěra and Josef Gočár) rivalled the German Bauhaus with their projects. A unique and original variation of architectural cubism developed by the likes of Pavel Janák and Josef Chochol also emerged in Prague.

Prague's immediate surroundings hold many places of artistic and historical importance. On the way to the White Mountain lies the Břevnov monastery, founded as long ago as 993 by St. Adalbert and the Czech Prince Boleslav. The baroque church is the work of Christopher Dientzenhofer and Brandl's paintings on the side altars are among the best of his extensive work. The White Mountain itself, in the shadow of the royal summer palace The Star, was the site of the Battle of the White Mountain which led to three hundred years of Habsburg rule. In the 18th century a place of pilgrimage was built on the battlefield with cloisters and the church of Our Lady Victorious to commemorate the victory of the imperial army that was achieved, according to legend, with the aid of the Virgin Mary. There are a number of Romanesque churches on the territory of Greater Prague, which prove how long it has been settled. They include the little Romanesque buildings in Dolní Chabry, Kyje and a basilica in Prosek. The church of All Saints in Slivenec is medieval in origin and contains a rare stained glass window dating from about 1370. On the southern edge of Prague lies the little town of Zbraslav, with a Cistercian monastery dating from the second half of the 13th century that served as the burial ground for the Bohemian kings on the model of the French Saint Denis. The cloisters and the baroque rooms of the prelature house the National Gallery's collections of Czech sculpture from the 19th and 20th centuries.

THE SURROUNDINGS OF PRAGUE

Many interesting day trips can be taken in the surroundings of Prague. On the highway from Prague to Brno and south Bohemia lies Průhonice castle, a historic building surrounded by a beautiful park dating from the 1880s. Part of the castle contains the Central Bohemian Gallery's collection of 20th century Czech art. Several dozen kilometres further on in the direction of Benešov, Konopiště castle hides in the woods. Its interior gives a picture of the life of the successor to the Austro-Hungarian throne, Franz Ferdinand d'Este, whose seat it was. The collection of hunting trophies is particularly remarkable, as are the statues and pictures of St. George from the archduke's own collection. The baroque castle of Jemniště, that used to belong to the Czech noble family of Šternberk, is also near Benešov. Its halls contain a wonderful collection of maps and pictures of European states and cities.

Kutná Hora, lying to the south east of Prague, was the most important town in the kingdom after Prague in the Middle Ages. It grew rich from mining silver and minting the coins of the kingdom. A number of churches and burghers' houses dating from the 13th to the 18th centuries have been restored. The 14th century church of St. Barbora, that both the Parléř workshop and Benedikt Rejt contributed to, looms over them. In the Gothic church of St. James Gothic fragments of altar arks have been preserved. Beside the Italian court are the workshops where coins were minted. The cistercian monastery in nearby Sedlec was one of the biggest monasteries in the country. Its monumental cathedral was rebuilt by Giovanni Santini in baroque Gothic style. The cemetary's charnal house holds decoratively arranged bones and skulls.

13 Not far from Kutná Hora is the little town of Kouřim, also important in the

Middle Ages. An outdoor museum near the town displays folk architecture from all over central and eastern Bohemia. Further down the road is Sázava, a little town dominated by a Benedictine monastery whose first abbot was St. Prokop, one of the patron saints of the Czech Lands. The foundations of a tetraconch rotunda from Romanesque times have recently been discovered in the monastery garden. Medieval paintings cover the walls of the capitular hall of the monastery, and in the convent there is an exhibition on the history of ancient Slavonic Sázava. On the Sázava river stands Český Šternberk castle, a building from the 13th century with interesting exhibitions of graphic works and weapons.

Going east from Prague we arrive at Stará Boleslav, home to the little Romanesque church of St. Kosmas and Damian and the basilica of St. Wenceslas, the core of which is Romanesque. The basilica stands where the Bohemian prince and patron saint, St. Wenceslas, was murdered in 935. The most revered picture of the Virgin Mary in Bohemia in the 17th and 18th centuries, a Marian relief known as the paladium of the Czech Lands, hangs in the pilgrim's church of Our Lady. In the area around Mělník we find the romantic Kokořín castle and a mansion in Liběchov containing the Náprstek Museum's collections of Asian art. Near the mansion, gigantic heads were carved into sandstone cliffs by the sculptor Václav Levý towards the middle of the 19th century. Mělník itself, the former dowry town of the Bohemian queens, lies above the meeting point of the two biggest Czech rivers, the Elbe and the Vltava. There is an exhibition of Czech baroque art in Mělník castle.

Just a few dozen kilometres north of Prague we find Nelahozeves castle, with its impressive collection of Czech and Spanish art from the 16th to the 18th centuries, most of which came from the Lobkowicz castle in Roudnice on the Elbe. The baroque mansion of Veltrusy with its romantic park also deserves a visit. Very near Prague lies the beautiful fortress of Roztoky in which exhibitions are now held. Inside the fort of Levý Hradec is the church of St. Clement, built atop the foundations of the oldest Christian shrine in Bohemia. Continuing northwards from here, we pass Říp Hill, a place wreathed in legends about the coming of the Bohemian tribe led by "Forefather Čech". On top of the hill is a Romanesque rotunda built by Prince Soběslav in 1126 on the site of an older wooden chapel. The Premonstratensian monastery in Doksany, not far from Říp Hill, also has Romanesque foundations. St. Agnes of Bohemia, a learned and spiritual member of the royal dynasty of Přemyslides in the 13th century, lived here in her youth. Altar statues and paintings by Czech baroque artists, including Petr Brandl and František Preiss, decorate the monastery church. Also in the vicinity are the Renaissance fort in Budyně, a baroque mansion with a beautiful garden in Libochovice, a ruined castle in Házmburk, and Terezín, a town that became tragically well known during the Second World War as a Jewish ghetto and concentration camp in which thousands of people from all over Europe perished. In Třebenice there is a museum of Bohemian garnets, a mineral abundant in the area; the exhibit includes the jewels that Goethe gave the young Ulrike von Levetzow.

On the road to Kladno and the west Bohemian spa towns is the village and mansion of Lány, the summer residence of the President of the Republic. The first president of the Czechoslovak Republic, T. G. Masaryk, lies buried in the little graveyard there. The royal castle of Křivoklát, with its beautiful interior, is hidden in deep forest.

Karlštejn Castle is one of Czechoslovakia's most visited sites and lies to the south west of Prague. Built in the middle of the 14th century by Charles IV, it is famous for the beautiful countryside that surrounds it and the splendid chapel of the Holy Rood, decorated with gold and semiprecious stones and containing medieval paintings by Master Theodoric.

Other trips can be made to Budeč, a fort with a Romanesque rotunda that is connected with the lives of St. Wenceslas and St. Ludmila, the ruins of Okoř castle and the outdoor museum of central Bohemian folk architecture in Přerov on the Elbe.

ILLUSTRATIONS

1/ Part of the City Reservation,
aerial view

3/ Prague Castle
and Malá Strana,
view from the Strahov garden

4/ Prague Castle
with St. Vitus' cathedral

5/ Prague Castle, St. George's basilica,
  interior

6/ St. George,
  National Gallery,
  St. George's Convent, 1373

7/ St. George's Convent, exhibition
of the National Gallery

8/ St. Matthew, Master Theodoric,
National Gallery, St. George's Convent,
before 1365

9/ Prague Castle, St. Vitus' cathedral
and the third courtyard

10/ Prague Castle, St. Vitus' cathedral,
flying buttresses, c. 1380

11/ Prague Castle,
St. Vitus' cathedral,
interior

12/ Prague Castle, St. Vitus' cathedral,
The Legend of Cyril and Methodius,
detail, Alphons Mucha's window, 1931

13/ Prague Castle, St. Vitus' cathedral,
stained glass window
with the Last Judgment,
Max Švabinský, 1937—1939

14/ Prague Castle, St. Vitus' cathedral,
    vaulting in the St. Wenceslas chapel,
    1362—1368

15/ Prague Castle,
    St. Vitus' cathedral,
    the Golden Gate,
    1366—1367

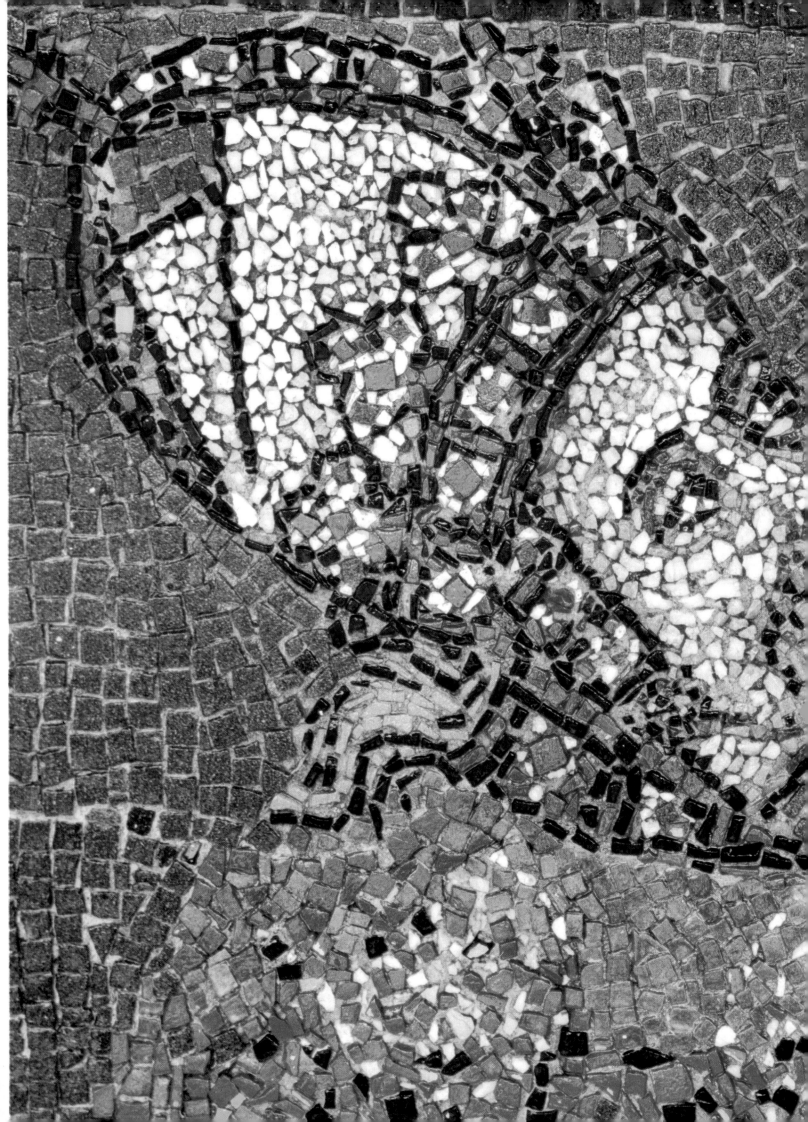

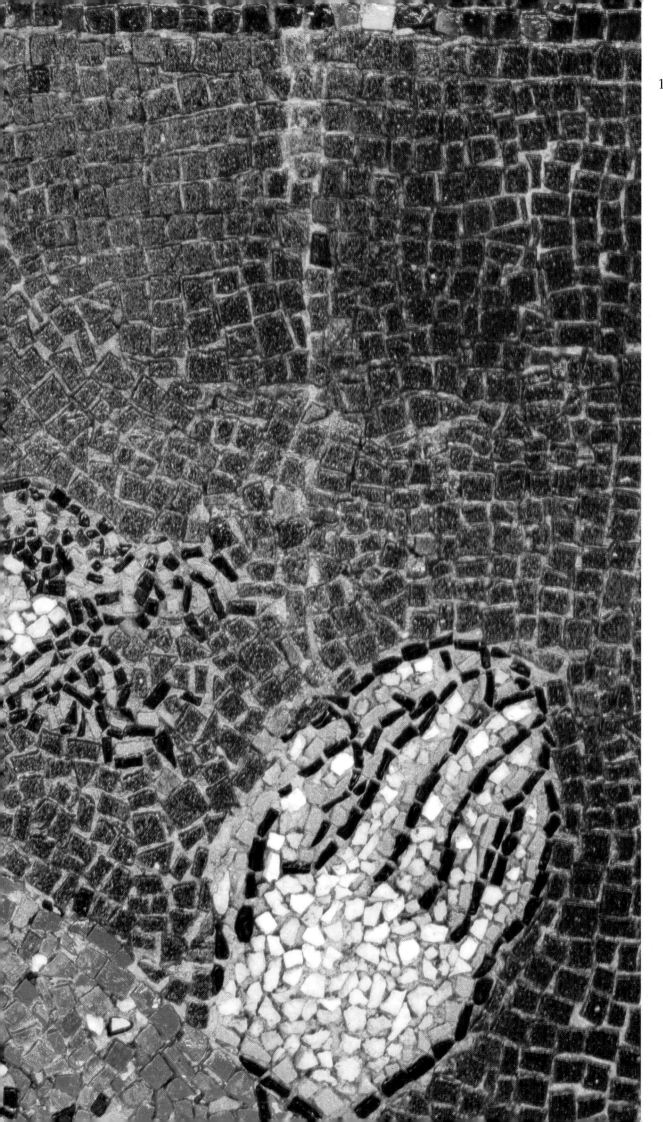

16/ Prague Castle,
St. Vitus'
cathedral,
detail of the
mosaic on the
Golden Gate

17/ Prague Castle, the St. Wenceslas' Crown, 1346

18/ Prague Castle, the Old Palace, the Hall of Wenceslas, c. 1400

19/ Prague Castle, bust of St. Vitus',
St. Vitus Treasure, before 1484

20/ Prague Castle,
St. Vitus' cathedral,
tomb of St. John of Nepomuk,
1733—1736

21/ Prague Castle,
   the Louis wing of the palace,
   1503—1510

22/ Prague Castle,
   the Riders' Steps,
   c. 1500

23/ Prague Castle, Matthias Gateway,
1614

24/ Prague Castle,
Golden Lane

25/ Prague Castle, Ball Court,
detail of the statue of Night
made in the workshop of M. B. Braun,
1734

26/ Prague Castle,
   the Royal summer palace (Belvedere),
   1538—1563

27/ Prague Castle, the Singing Fountain
   near the Royal summer palace (Belvedere),
   detail, 1564—1568

28/ The Picture Gallery of Prague Castle

29/ The Young Lady at her Toilette, Tizian,
Picture Gallery of Prague Castle,
probably 1515

30/ Portrait of Mrs Schreyvogel,
Jan Kupecký,
Picture Gallery of Prague Castle,
c. 1716

31/ The Šternberk palace in Hradčany,
National Gallery exhibition

32/ The gardens
of Prague Castle,
music pavilion

33/ Garden of the
Černín palace
with its orangery

34/ Hradčany Square

35/ Archbishop's palace
in Hradčany Square,
late 18th century

36/ Archbishop's palace
in Hradčany Square,
interior

37/ Martinic palace
in Hradčany Square,
second half of 16th century

38/ Martinic palace
in Hradčany Square,
Renaissance ceiling, detail

39/ Hradčany and Loretto Square,
aerial view

40/ Hradčany Lane

41/ The Loretto at Hradčany,
Santa Casa, 1626—1631

42/ The Lobkowicz monstrance
in the Loretto Treasure,
1673

43/ Strahov monastery,
aerial view

44/ The Strahov Library,
Philosophical Hall,
1782—1784

45/ Gate Na Pískách in Hradčany,
1721

46/ The Town Hall Steps,
Hradčany

48/ The roofs of Malá Strana

49/ Malá Strana palaces

50/ House At the Two Suns
in Nerudova Street,
detail

51/ Baroque house
At the Three Little Fiddles
in Nerudova Street,
detail

52/ Nerudova Street in Malá Strana,
upper part

53/ Malá Strana, Valdštejn palace, aerial view

54/ Malá Strana, aerial view

55/ Malá Strana,
view from the dome
of the church
of St. Nicholas

56/ St. Nicholas' church with
the roofs of Malá Strana

57/ St. Nicholas' church
in Malá Strana, 1703—1755

58/ St. Nicholas' church,
dome, 1737—1752 > >

59/ St. Nicholas' church,
organ, 1745—1746 > > >

60/ Valdštejn garden
in Malá Strana, 1627

62/ Valdštejn palace in Malá Strana, great hall

61/ Valdštejn palace
in Malá Strana, 1624—1630

63/ Malá Strana gardens

64/ The Vrtba garden
in Malá Strana,
after 1720

65/ The Lobkowicz palace

66/ St. Thomas' church
in Malá Strana,
high altar, 1731

67/ The Palace of the Grand Prior
of the Order of the Maltese Cross (Johannites)
in Malá Strana, exhibition
of the Music Museum,
1726—1731

68/ Kinský summer palace in Smíchov,
1827—1831

69/ The Bertramka House in Smíchov

70/ Hope, copy of the statue by M. B. Braun,
Malá Strana Metro station,
1718—1719

71/ Houses on the
Čertovka stream,
Malá Strana >

72/ The Čertovka > >

73/ Maltese church
of Our Lady "Below-the-Chain",
Malá Strana

74/ House At the Three Ostriches
in Malá Strana, 1585

75/ Romanesque relief
in Malá Strana, c. 1170,
detail

76/ Charles Bridge,
aerial view

77/ Charles Bridge with the building on the Old Town bridge head

78/ Charles Bridge
with the statue
of the Calvary

79/ View from Malá Strana
to the Old Town

80/ Square of the Knights
of the Cross
in the Old Town,
aerial view

81/ Old Town Bridge Tower,
Peter Parléř,
end of 14th century

82/ Charles Bridge with the
church of St. Francis Seraph
in the Old Town

83/ Fresco with the Last Judgment
in the church of St. Francis Seraph,
V. V. Reiner, detail, 1722—1723

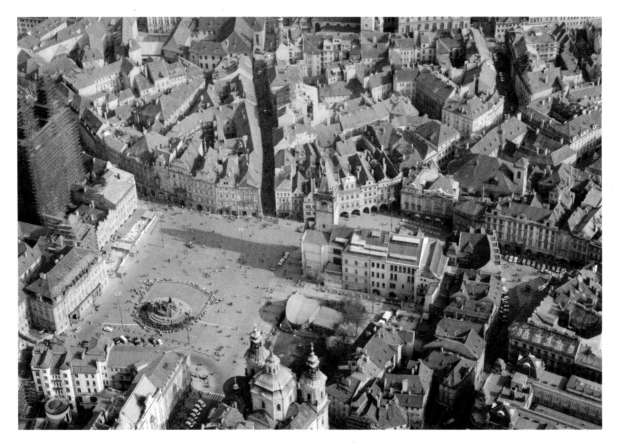

84/ The Old Town Square,
aerial view

85/ The Old Town,
aerial view

86/ View of the Old Town
from Letná

87/ The Clementinum in the Old Town,
detail of the Astronomical Tower,
1721—1723

88/ The Clementinum
and the Clam-Gallas Palace
in the Old Town

89/ House At the Golden Serpent
in the Old Town,
Karlova Street

90/ Building of the
    Old Town Hall

91/ The emblem
    of the
    City of Prague
    on the
    Old Town Hall

92/ House At the Minute,
Old Town Square,
end of 16th century

93/ The Old Town Hall

94/ The Jan Hus monument
on the Old Town Square,
Ladislav Šaloun,
detail, 1900—1915

95/ Old Town Square,
eastern side

97/ Romanesque hall in Husova Street
in the Old Town,
12th century

96/ The Holy Rood rotunda in the Old Town,
end of 11th century

98/ The Holy Rood rotunda
in the Old Town,
neo-romanesque grating
from the year 1862

99/ Romanesque painting in the Old Town,
middle of 13th century

100/ House of the Squires of Kunštát
in the Old Town, 12th century

101/ Tower of Old Town fortifications,
first half of 13th century

102/ House At the Golden Well
in the Old Town

103/ The Carolinum in the Old Town,
facade

104/ The Carolinum in the Old Town, main hall

105/ The Bethlehem chapel,
Old Town

106/ Havelská street
in the Old Town,
arcades

107/ The well with Renaissance
lattice-work on Malé náměstí,
1560

108/ Agnes Convent,
the cloister

109/ Morning, Josef Mánes,
National Gallery,
Agnes Convent, 1857

110/ Agnes Convent, exhibition of the National Gallery

111/ Agnes Convent, ground floor

112/ Church of St. Gastulus
in the Old Town,
console, after 1375

113/ Church of St. Gastulus
in the Old Town,
northern nave, after 1375

114/ Church of St. James
in the Old Town,
relief on the facade,
c. 1695

115/ Church of St. James in the Old Town,
Ferdinand Maxmilián Brokof,
the tomb of Václav Vratislav of Mitrovice
1714—1716

<<< 116/ The Old-New Synagogue in Josefov, 1270

<< 117/ The Old-New Synagogue, entrance hall,
early 14th century

118/ Memorial plaque to Franz Kafka
in the Old Town, 1964—1966

119/ The Jewish Museum in Josefov,
exhibition of childern's
drawings

120/ Temple curtain, Jewish Museum, 1592

121/ The Old Jewish cemetery
     in Josefov, detail of tombs

122/ Moses, František Bílek,
     Old Town, 1905

123/ The Smetana Museum
in the Old Town, 1883

124/ Stavovské divadlo
(the Estates Theatre)
in the Old Town, 1781—1783

125/ The Municipal House of the City of Prague
in the Old Town, 1903—1911

126/ The Municipal House of the City of Prague
in the Old Town, grating

127/ The House of Artists in the Old Town,
interior, 1876—1884

128/ The Kiss,
Josef Mařatka,
Petřín Park, 1910

129/ The Allegory
of the Vltava,
Václav Prachner,
1812, Old Town

130/ Cubist houses
in the Old Town,
1919—1921

131/ House At the Black Mother of God,
Old Town, stairway, 1911—1912

132/ The New Town,
aerial view

133/ Wenceslas Square in the New Town,
aerial view

134/ Wenceslas Square in the New Town

135/ The National Museum,
Pantheon, 1885—1890 >

136/ The St. Wenceslas
monument on Wenceslas Square,
J. V. Myslbek, 1887—1922 >>

137/ Hotel Europa
on Wenceslas Square,
detail, 1903—1905

138/ Cubist candelabrum
in the New Town, 1912

139/ St. Longine's rotunda
in the New Town, second
half of 12th century

140/ House At the Iberians
on Republic Square

141/ The Franciscan garden
with the church
of Our Lady of the Snows,
New Town

142/ St. Stephen's church,
New Town,
second half
of 14th century

143/ Church of the Most Holy Heart
of the Lord in Vinohrady,
Josip Plečnik, 1932

144/ The National Theatre, New Town,
1868—1883

145/ The National Theatre,
auditorium

146/ The National Theatre,
salon of the
President's Box

147/ Society building
on Slavonic Island,
1830—1837

148/ The River Vltava
and the Mánes building
in the New Town

149/ Charles Square,
     aerial view

150/ The New Town Hall,
     1377—1418

151/ Faust House in Charles Square,
second half of 16th century

152/ Church of Our Lady on the Lawn,
New Town, after 1360

153/ The Emmaus church, facade >>

154/ Emmaus monastery,
mural painting, c. 1370 >>>

<< 155/ The summer palace of Michna of Vacínov (Amerika),
   New Town, 1712—1720

<< 156/ Church of Our Lady and Charlemagne at Karlov,
   New Town

 < 157/ Church of Our Lady and Charlemagne at Karlov,
   vaulting

158/ Vyšehrad, aerial view

159/ The River Vltava with Vyšehrad Castle

160/ St. Martin's rotunda at Vyšehrad,
end of 11th century

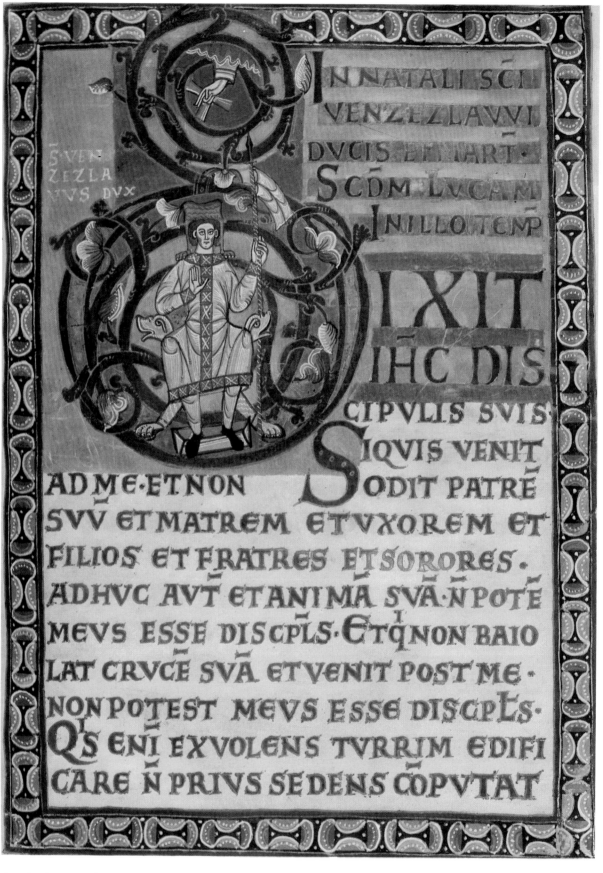

161/ The Vyšehrad Codex,
page with the initial D,
c. 1085

162/ Tile form,
St. Lawrence's basilica
at Vyšehrad, c. 1130

164/ The villa of the Čapek brothers in Vinohrady, 1923—1925

165/ Cubist apartment
house below
Vyšehrad,
1913—1914

163/ Ctirad a Šárka,
statue
on Palacký Bridge,
Vyšehrad,
J. V. Myslbek,
1881—1895

166/ The National Technical Museum in Holešovice,
central hall, 1936—1941

167/ Saloon dining car, interior,
National Technical Museum, 1891

168/ Stromovka Park
and the Governor's summer palace

169/ The Chateau at Libeň,
second half of 18th century

172/ Romanesque basilica
of St. Václav in Prosek,
11th or 12th century

173/ The Church of Cyril
and Methodius in Karlín,
1854—1863

< 170/ The Baba residential area,
1928—1940

< 171/ Baroque homestead
at Bohnice, 1777

174/ The Church of All Saints at Slivenec,
end of 13th century

175/ The Church of All Saints at Slivenec,
window, detail, c. 1370

177/ Pilgrims' church of Our Lady Victorious
on the White Mountain,
1704—1730

178/ Chodov, a former fort

< 176/ The Star summer palace in the park
on the White Mountain, aerial view

179/ Romanesque church of St. John the Baptist
in Dolní Chabry, third quarter
of 12th century

180/ Church of St. Margaret
with the Benedictine monastery
in Břevnov, 1708—1715

181/ The Zlíchov church
and Braník

182/ Trója baroque
summer palace,
1679

183/ Trója summer palace,
murals by
Abraham and Isaac Godyn,
1688—1697

184/ The Chateau at Troja,
detail of the stairways,
1685—1703

187/ The Chateau at Zbraslav,
exhibition of statues by J. Štursa

188/ The Chateau at Zbraslav,
Humanity, Jan Štursa, detail,
1911—1913,
National Gallery

< 185/ Zbraslav, aerial view

< 186/ The Chateau at Zbraslav,
exhibition of the
National Gallery

189/ Neo-renaissance mansion
and park in Průhonice,
1889—1894

190/ Konopiště castle, former seat
of the Austrian archduke,
Franz Ferdinand d'Este,
rebuilt at the end of 19th century

191/ Baroque castle of Jemniště, 1724

192/ Premonstratensian monastery in Doksany, baroque restoration from the end of 17th to the third quarter of 18th century

193/ Baroque castle in Veltrusy
with its classicist park,
second decade of 18th century

194/ Renaissance castle in Nelahozeves,
1553—1600, exhibition of ancient art
from the collections of the Central
Bohemian Gallery

195/ The Romanesque rotunda of St. George
     on Říp hill, 1126

196/ Liběchov castle, first half of 18th century,
     containing collections of Asian art
     from the Náprstek Museum

197/ Devils' heads, Václav Levý,
     Liběchov, 1844—1845

198/ Lány mansion, summer residence
of the President of the Republic

199/ Baroque castle of Dobříš,
1745—1765

200/ Kokořín castle, reconstructed
in romantic style in 1911—1918

201/ Křivoklát castle, the core
dating from 13th century

202/ Kouřim, outdoor museum of folk architecture

203/ A baroque place of pilgrimage with the church of Our Lady, Svatá Hora (Holy Hill) near Příbram, 1658—1709

204/ Český Šternberk castle, the interiors mainly from 17th century

205/ Romanesque basilica
of the Assumption
of the Virgin Mary in Tismice,
third quarter of 12th century

206/ Karlštejn castle,
the most beautiful
Czech medieval castle,
1348—1355

207/ Former Benedictine monastery,
Sázava, founded 1032

TABLE OF ILLUSTRATIONS

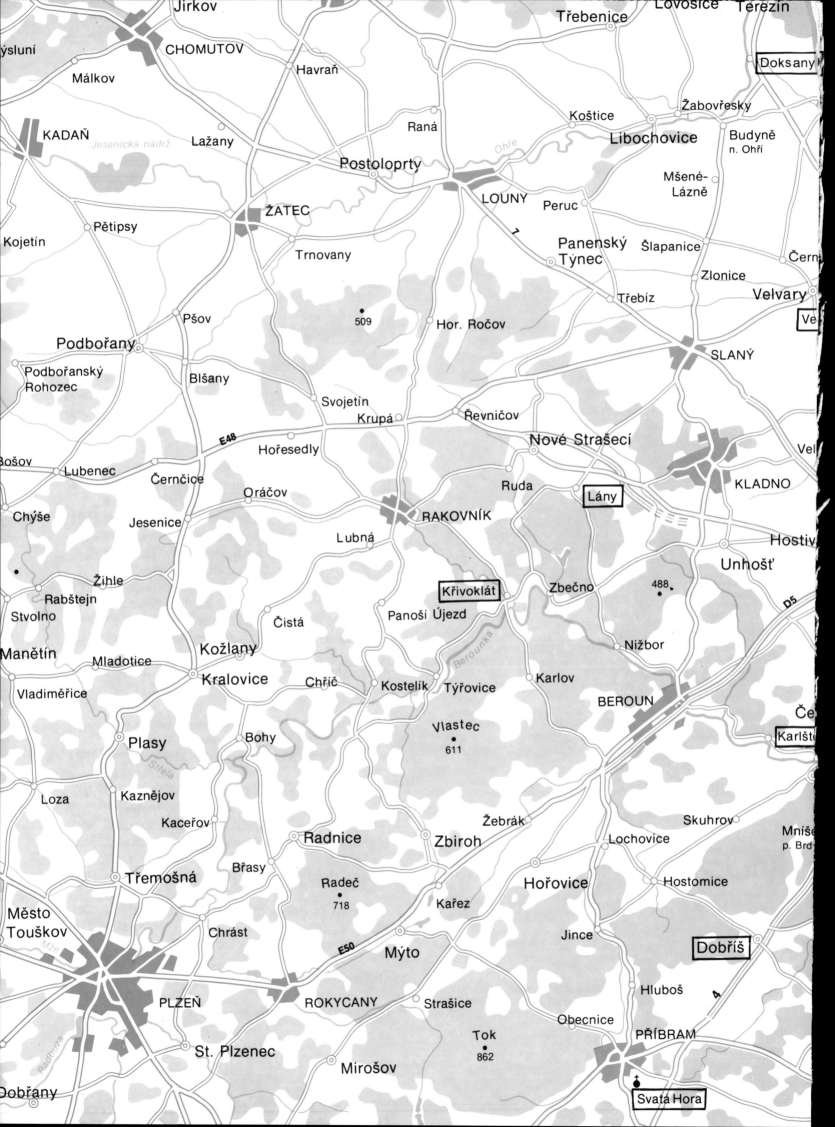